# Success Secrets from the Bible

Biblical Principles for Success

Kenneth Mwale

© Copyright 2017 Kenneth Mwale

All rights reserved.

No part of this book may be reproduced or utilised in any form, or by any means, electronic or mechanical, without written permission from the individual author and the publisher.

All scripture quotes are from either the New International Version of the Bible, The New King James Version, or The Good News Bible unless otherwise stated.

Published by Practical Truth Library

Tel: 0724236990

kenmwale@gmail.com

www.kennethmwale.com

## Dedication

**Dedication**

This book is dedicated to Jesus the author and finisher of my success.

To Rabecca, Jethro, and Jemimah who I consider my reasons for success.

To all my friends and my Doxa Deo family, especially those at Berea campus who gave me a shot at success.

# Contents

| | |
|---|---|
| Preface | 1 |
| Introduction: Courage and Humility | 2 |
| Chapter 1<br>Secret #1; Add Value | 9 |
| Chapter 2<br>Secret #2; Marry the King's Daughter at the right time | 21 |
| Chapter 3<br>Secret #3; Mind Your Own Business | 33 |
| Chapter 4<br>Secret #4; Be Curious | 51 |
| Chapter 5<br>Secret #5 Know what you bring to the deal | 61 |
| Chapter 6<br>Secret #6; Action Precedes Learning | 75 |
| Chapter 7<br>Secret #7; Man cannot live on bread alone | 83 |
| Chapter 8<br>Secret #8; You are a Hebrew | 93 |
| Chapter 9<br>Secret #9; Aim for Retirement | 103 |

## Preface

Google defines the word secret as something "not known or seen or not meant to be known or seen by others". The second meaning is "something that is kept or meant to be kept unknown or unseen by others". This is what is commonly known as a secret. I do not disagree with these definitions at all. We tell people that we are holding a surprise party for someone which should be kept a secret. In other words, until the day the party will be held, this party remains a secret to the person in whose honour it will be held.

I, however, want to use the word in another way. The word secret has a secondary meaning, and that is what I am using in this book. The word secret may mean something hidden and not to be made known but can also mean something that is a key ingredient to something else, or something central to a process without which that thing or process is nothing.

For example, someone would say, the secret to success is consistency. When the word is used in this fashion, it doesn't mean that consistency should be kept unknown and hidden. This simply means that for anyone to succeed they should keep doing something over and over for a long time. Consistency is central to the process and without it, success would not happen. This is how I use the word in this book.

Success secrets from the Bible are not those things that are hidden and should be kept that way. Not at all. I am talking about those things that one can do to guarantee success in their life. I list nine such principles. Each one stands alone. You do not have to do all nine. Everyone's circumstances are different, therefore what may work for someone may not be what works for you. You need to look at which secret would apply to your situation and apply it

I hope and pray these secrets will help you achieve the success you are dreaming about. God bless you on your journey towards your success.

## Introduction: Courage and Humility

*Be strong and of good courage, for to this people you shall [a]divide as an inheritance the land which I swore to their fathers to give them. ⁷ Only be strong and very courageous, that you may observe to do according to all the law which Moses My servant commanded you; do not turn from it to the right hand or to the left, that you may [b]prosper wherever you go. ⁸ This Book of the Law shall not depart from your mouth, but you[c] shall meditate in it day and night, that you may observe to do according to all that is written in it. For then you will make your way prosperous, and then you will have good success. ⁹ Have I not commanded you? Be strong and of good courage; do not be afraid, nor be dismayed, for the Lord your God is with you wherever you go."*[1]

When someone wants to emphasize a point they usually repeat it several times. In the above

---

[1] Joshua 1:6-9

scripture, the word courage appears several times. God emphasizes the need for courage as a leader, but it is not only for leaders. It is also for everyone who wants to achieve anything in life.

The reason courage is required to achieve success is because coping out is easy. Giving excuses is our number one deterrent to success. Fear of what other people may think of us for doing things different is the biggest of our fears. It terrifies most people to be different and as a result they won't do what they must do for fear of censure from other people. Courage helps us to overcome the fear of "what will people think of me?"

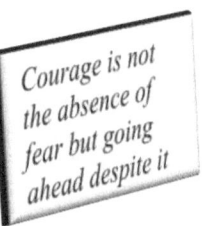
*Courage is not the absence of fear but going ahead despite it*

Another common concern is the fear of saying no to what must be denied and yes to what should be accepted. Most people find it hard to say no to things that they know hinder their success. Other people find it hard to say yes to what they need if that involves looking different from the crowd.

## Kenneth Mwale

Courage is not the absence of fear but going ahead despite it. Courageous people are just as afraid as everyone else. The difference is that courageous people act despite their fear. There is no need for courage if fear is not present. The fact that we need courage means that fear does not go away, we have to act despite its presence.

Courage is the antidote of fear. If we allow what needs to be denied and deny what needs to be allowed, success eludes us. It takes courage to say yes sometimes, and it takes even more courage to say no. Everyone wants to be successful but it takes courage to be successful.

Courage is one thing. But there is also one other ingredient just as important to success. Humility.

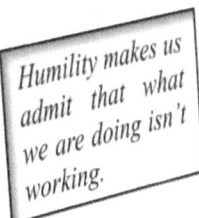

*Humility makes us admit that what we are doing isn't working.*

Courage helps us do things that may scare the day lights out of some people. Humility makes us admit that what we are doing isn't working. It takes a lot of humility to admit we are on the wrong road. Because people lack humility, they can continue on a wrong path just to prove a point. A humble man or woman admits when they are wrong and stop what they are doing.

Therefore, to succeed we need to be both humble and courageous. Courage makes us do the things that scare others but are necessary to do. Humility helps us stop doing what isn't working to concentrate on what needs to be done. These two concepts work hand in hand. It also takes humility to accept when we don't know something and we need to learn. It takes humility to accept failure and start again.

In the book of revelation, we see a picture that seem to be contradictory. A scene unfolds where John the Revelator is troubled when there is no one courageous enough to open the scroll. The Holy Spirit told him that the Lion of the tribe of Judah was worthy to open the scroll. What was strange was when John looked at the one worthy to open the scroll, instead of seeing a lion, he saw a lamb. Not just a lamb, but one that looked like it was slain.

## Kenneth Mwale

*And no man in heaven, nor in earth, neither under the earth, was able to open the book, neither to look thereon. And I wept much, because no man was found worthy to open and to read the book, neither to look thereon. And one of the elders saith unto me, Weep not: behold, the Lion of the tribe of Juda, the Root of David, hath prevailed to open the book, and to loose the seven seals thereof. And I beheld, and, lo, in the midst of the throne and of the four beasts, and in the midst of the elders, stood a Lamb as it had been slain, having seven horns and seven eyes, which are the seven Spirits of God sent forth into all the earth*[2].

This is a picture of people that become successful. They have this contradiction. They have a lot of fire inside them, but when we look at them they look like a lamb. They don't have the outer physical features of a lion, but that of a lamb, but they have hearts of a lion. When we are in their company they are normal people. It is when a situation requiring courage

---

[2] Revelation 5:3-6

comes up that we start to see that they are not just lambs after all. They have a side to them that is fierce.

The chapters that follow build on these two concepts. Some of the Bible's secrets of success have to do with the courage it takes to be successful. Other secrets are offshoots of humility. Stay with me as we look at each of the Success Secrets from the Bible.

## Chapter 1

## Success Secret #1: Add Value

*"Now you Philippians know also that in the beginning of the gospel, when I departed from Macedonia, no church shared with me concerning giving and receiving but you only"*[3].

Now you GIVING and RECEIVING is at the heart of any success story. What we give is what we get back out of life. If we are not happy with our life, look at what we are giving. When I say giving, I am not talking about what has commonly come to be known as "seed" type of giving. I am not talking about giving offerings. I am talking about giving something of value to society. We need to give something that society VALUES. Success is guaranteed when we figure out what our immediate environment is in need of.

---

[3] Philippians 4:15

Giving and receiving is also shown in our attitude, not just in physical things. A person that has an attitude of a giver always looks for how they can add value to other people's lives. They do not just wait for society to give them something but always look for what they can give to society. As a result, society in turn gives them back something of value. It can be money or something intangible like respect or honor.

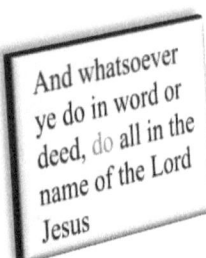
And whatsoever ye do in word or deed, do all in the name of the Lord Jesus

What most people don't know is that their workplace needs value adding people. When we put ourselves in a giving mode in our workplace, the superiors notice. If they don't, someone who does business with our workplace will notice. But if any of these two don't notice, there is someone even more important who will notice and always rewards a giver, and that is God Himself.

## Kenneth Mwale

*"And whatsoever ye do in word or deed, do all in the name of the Lord Jesus, giving thanks to God and the Father by him[4]".*

There two things that are very important about value. The first is the amount of value we put out there. When we give small amounts of value, small amounts of value come to us. If we give vast amounts of value, vast amounts of value come to us. Two passages of scripture reveal this truth.

*"love ye your enemies, and do good, and lend, hoping for nothing again; and your reward shall be great, and ye shall be the children of the Highest: for he is kind unto the unthankful and to the evil. Be ye therefore merciful, as your Father also is merciful. Judge not, and ye shall not be judged: condemn not, and ye shall not be condemned: forgive, and ye shall be forgiven: Give, and it shall be given unto you; good measure, pressed down, and shaken together, and running over, shall men give into your bosom. For with*

---

[4] Colossians 3:17

*the same measure that ye mete withal it shall be measured to you again[5]*".

This passage of scripture is usually used for giving money. When we consider the context in which this scripture find itself, we see that the giving mentioned has very little to do with money. Jesus is revealing a principle about giving more than He is talking about money. He started this discussion with a generalisation that if we do good we get a reward. He then comes to specific things like giving forgiveness and not having a judgemental attitude.

What the Lord shows us here is that giving is a principle. If we give anything of value, in return we receive something of value. When we have an attitude that loves to give, we in turn receive from the Lord through people something of value. It may not always be something physical, but we always receive when we give.

The scripture however reveals very emphatically that the amounts of value we give determines the

---

[5] Luke 6:35-38

amounts we get back. Although the amounts come multiplied, truth is, a small amount multiplied results into something small, and a big amount results into a big result.

Another scripture that shows us that we need to give more is Matthew 20:26.

*"Yet it shall not be so among you; but whoever desires to become great among you, let him be your servant. 27 And whoever desires to be first among you, let him be your slave— 28 just as the Son of Man did not come to be served, but to serve, and to give His life a ransom for many.[6]"*

When we figure out what value to add to society, our next step is to find out how we can scale up the distribution of that value to touch more people with it. When we just leave it to giving without figuring out the distribution channels to get it to many people, we may not gain much from our value. What we need is to create a system that creates, duplicates and distributes

---

[6] Matthew 20:26

our value to touch as many people as we possibly can. When we perfect this system of producing, multiplying or duplicating and distributing that which we value brings more value to us. . Value that does not reach people is not valuable.

The Lord, in the scriptures above, revealed a great principle when He said that he came to give His life *"a ransom to many"*. This is what it is all about. We should give our value to many not just a few, and we will be a success.

It is not just that value should be more in quantity. The quality of value affects continued flow of value back to us. If we want to have a continuous flow of value, we must make sure we put out high quality value. We cannot cut corners and think that what we give continues to produce value for us. We may have figured out how to distribute our value, however, sustainability comes from the quality of our value.

The Bible is not quiet about this. *"Do you see a man who excels in his work? He will stand before kings; He will not stand before unknown men"*[7].

---

[7] Proverbs 22:29

To insure continuity of value coming our way, give high quality value. The Bible says if we do we will even serve kings. What that means is that our value attracts the high-quality people of society, and we know that when that happens, we get high quality value back. The quality of value determines the quality of people we serve. The quality of people we serve determines the quality of value we receive back and the continuity thereof.

What separates extraordinary performers from the ordinary is not what they do, it is how they do it. High-quality people provide high-quality value. They do not just produce more. They produce more high-quality value.

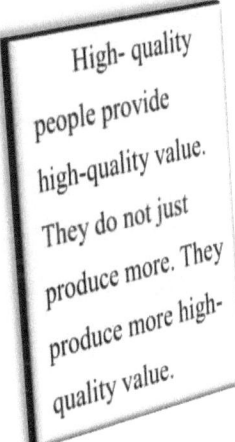

There are three important factors to consider if we want to reach more people with our value and when we want to also produce high-quality.

These three things help us reach more people and to raise the quality of our value.

### Excel at What You Do

*"But as you abound in everything—in faith, in speech, in knowledge, in all diligence, and in your love for us—see that you abound in this grace also[8]."*

This passage provides great advice about value. If we want to succeed, make sure we become good at what we do. Let us cultivate the discipline of getting better every day. Let us improve our craft and become sought after people in our fields of expertise. We need to excel at what we do for it to increase in value.

### Actively Work at Making Our Work a Success

*"And seek the peace of the city where I have caused you to be carried away captive, and pray to the Lord for it; FOR IN ITS PEACE YOU WILL HAVE PEACE[9].*

---

[8] 2 Corinthians 8:7
[9] Jeremiah 29:7

There is a popular saying which says, "don't kill the goose that lays the golden eggs". This is such a true saying which most people violate. If we work for someone, or for a company, or the government, what we need to do is make sure that we u work for the success of that enterprise.

Isn't it ironic that people steal from their work but still think their company will survive? They steal resources and time from their job or business and expect it won't have a negative effect on the company. Remember, if we work at the success of our source of income, our source of income gives us more.

**Know The State of Your Flock**

*"Be diligent to know the state of your flocks, And attend to your herds.*[10]

If we want to succeed at anything, we need to be so in touch with the state of affairs of our career or business. A good eye for detail helps to produce success. We need to know what is going on in our field

---

[10] Proverbs 23:27

of expertise, otherwise we work hard, but one day we may find that we are irrelevant.

A good eye for detail helps to produce success.

    Success secret number one is value adding. Find what society needs and give it. Don't just give a little. Give more. Nonetheless, don't just give more, give more high-quality value. When we do this we are on our way to success.

    On the other hand, make sure that we sharpened our axe, so we can cut better. Let's get better at what we do. Let us work at making our vehicle for success a success. Don't kill the goose that lays our golden eggs. Lastly, be diligent and always be on alert about what is going on in our industry because if we don't, we'll work hard and find that our value is valueless.

## Chapter 2

## Success Secret #2: Marry the King's Daughter at the right time

I begin this chapter with a story from one of my favorite characters from the Bible, David. The scriptural references below capture the story.

*"And Saul said to David, Behold my elder daughter Merab, her will I give thee to wife: only be thou valiant for me, and fight the LORD'S battles. For Saul said, Let not mine hand be upon him, but let the hand of the Philistines be upon him. And David said unto Saul, Who am I? and what is my life, or my father's family in Israel, that I should be son in law to the king?*[11]

*"And David also sent messengers to Ishbosheth to say, "Give me back my wife Michal. I paid a hundred Philistine foreskins in order to marry*

---

[11] 1 Samuel 18:17-18

*her." So Ishbosheth had her taken from her husband Paltiel son of Laish. Paltiel followed her all the way to the town of Bahurim, crying as he went. But when Abner said, "Go back home," he did.*[12]

 

The strange thing in these two passages is that in the first, David refused to marry the King's daughter. However, we see that when he becomes king in chapter 2, among the first things he does is to ask for the woman he refused to marry a few years back.

I have always asked myself questions about this story. Why did David refuse the King's daughter the first time? And why would he get her when he becomes King, even when she was someone's wife by this time? The fact that he had to go after her, even after she was someone's wife, means that even at the time he refused to marry her, he still wanted her.

The answer to these questions holds secret number two on our path to success. The secret is we should marry the King's daughter at the right time. I

---

[12] 2 Samuel 3:14

am sure you are asking what in the world is marrying the King's daughter at the right time?

*I believe even though David refused the King's daughter the first time around, he really fancied to be the King's son in-law, and he loved the King's daughter too.*

I believe even though David refused the King's daughter the first time around, he really fancied to be the King's son in-law, and he loved the King's daughter too. The problem was that at the time David was a common soldier in King Saul's army. He realized marrying the King's daughter would be more a liability than anything else. Marrying the King's daughter at this time would spell trouble for David.

Why? Because when the King's daughter was given to him, David was not able to maintain the lifestyle that the King's daughter was used to. Instead of her being a blessing to him, she would be a burden. The King's daughter was used to a certain way of life. That life was way beyond what David could provide. If he married her, he would have to spend more than he could afford and incur debt. Therefore, David figured, although it would be great to be a King's son-in-law, practically it was beyond him. Although he loved the girl, he declined marrying her.

David chose a wise path, even if marrying from the royal family was such a cool thing. He resisted the temptation. David realized that yes, people would look at him as a great guy who was the King's son-in-law. But deep down in his heart, he would be living a lie because he had no resources to maintain her. He would in turn be living a life that wasn't authentic.

This happens to a lot of people. They show a flashy lifestyle that they have at a cost. They drive cars they cannot afford. They lay in houses they cannot afford. They are riddled with bad debt all in the name of being the "King's sons-in-laws". By the way, this is an illustration that also applies to women.

Being a King's son-in-law is just a figurative way of saying we are 'living the life'. We have at our disposal all that life offers. We ride royal horses, stay in royal courts rubbing shoulders with the cream of the Israeli society. But inside, David knew all that was not because of him, but because of a marriage to the daughter of the King.

David wanted to wait until marrying the King's daughter was going to be something he would do not as a favor, but because he deserved it. He didn't want to derive his importance from the marriage to the King's daughter, but to what he achieved. The King's daughter would be a wife to him just like anyone else. He would only derive his importance from his achievement as a person, not a marriage.

The danger of marrying the King's daughter at the wrong time is that she becomes a hindrance to our personal success. We would continually live under her shadow. Most people live like that. They derive their importance from the things they flash, even if those things are acquired at such a high cost like debt or a life compromise. They do everything to show off even if it means compromise, or selling out to true joy.

Success comes to people who delay gratification. Success comes to people who are not pressured to buy or acquire things they don't need. Success favors people who have the emotional maturity to live within their means and not above just to impress others.

There are people that buy cars on-hire purchase and use more than half of their salary to pay the installment. Not because they cannot buy a

> Success comes to people who delay gratification. Success comes to people who are not pressured to buy or acquire things they don't need.

car that is within their affordability. They do it to show off. They live a lie because while everyone thinks they have arrived. The truth is every month they live under the pressure of paying for their over-the-top car, because they also have other obligations. Such people go to lengths living a flashy lifestyle, not for themselves, but so people can say, hey, look at that son-in-law of the King.

Marrying the King's daughter at the right time simply means that we live within our means. We buy things we can afford. We go on holidays we can afford and take our kids to schools that are within our means.

Instead of marrying the King's daughter and using her to derive your importance, the better way is to work hard and earn your way. Aim at earning more, but live within your means. While you should have big dreams, don't live the dreams before the dream comes to pass. David wanted the King's daughter, but he waited until it was the right time for him to have her. He didn't succumb to the pressure of what people would think of him if he wasn't the son-in-law of the King. He knew if he worked himself up, one day he would be a worthy King's son-in-law. The good thing is that when that day came, being the son-in-law of the King was not something from where he derived his worth. He was a King himself so being another King's son-in-law was nothing.

There are two problems with marrying the King's daughter at wrong time. The first is that we blow our chances of future financial success because we are always behind on our financial obligations. We will always play catch up on our bills and we cannot save money to start building another stream of income. Money is a good slave but can become a very ruthless master if we allow it to control us. People controlled by money live very stressful lives because they are always trying to cover up their financial deficiencies by incurring more debt, and some even succumb to doing wrong things.

Another problem with this way of living is it is not authentic. People who make such decisions make them to cover up their own low self-esteem. They use outward things like cars, houses, or other material things to cover up their sadness. Problem is, things cannot replace an authentic feeling of self-worth. Either we feel worth irrespective of what we have, or don't have, or we don't. Success favors people who know how to delay gratification and who don't live for other people. Live an authentic life.

**Standard of Living and Quality**

The antidote for a life of pleasing people and the need to impress is to know the difference between quality of life and standard of living. These two concepts become critical to living a life of personal freedom. There are a lot of people who are not living for themselves but for other people. They are more interested in what people will think of them than how they feel. They accept huge debts to impress even when it is hard to pay back. They are unhappy but cannot change because their feeling of worth does not come from inside but from what other people say or think about them.

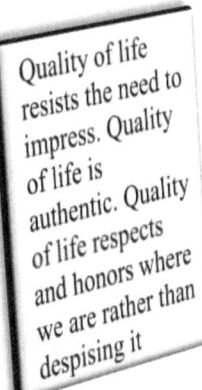

Quality of life resists the need to impress. Quality of life is authentic. Quality of life respects and honors where we are rather than despising it

Standard of living is what society imposes on us as a benchmark of what success is. Society tells us what a successful person looks like. But is success about what others think it is, or what we say it is? If the world considers living in a big house and driving a big car as success, will we kill ourselves to get those even when we can't afford them at the time? Instead of working hard to get those things at the right time when we can afford them, most people end up marrying the King's daughter before they are ready.

Quality of life on the other hand is different. Quality of life doesn't look at what society prescribes. Quality of life looks at where one is and how one lives within their means based on what makes them happy.

Quality of life resists the need to impress. Quality of life is authentic. Quality of life respects and honors where we are rather than despising it. Quality of life looks at what makes us happy within what we have, not on what makes others happy, even if it is outside what we can afford.

I love quality of life because it doesn't find happiness outside me as a person. It finds happiness within me and within what I have and can afford. It is that way of living that only cares about authenticity, not the fake outside world. It is not trying to please people we don't know, who don't even care.

**Personal Target Lifestyle**

What has helped our family to stay grounded and resist the pressure to impress and marry the King's daughter before time? It is something I developed and call a Personal Targeted Lifestyle, or PTL. PTL is a personally decided lifestyle target that we set as an individual or a family. This is something we do irrespective of what the world sets as a standard.

PTL sets boundaries for you and your family. This insulates you from the pressure of wanting to impress and live for others. Instead, you live on your terms and define success on your terms. People with a PTL can resist the temptation of marrying the King's daughter before time, because they are not driven by outside pressures but by their own decisions based on what they set as a target for how they want to live.

## Chapter 3

## Success Secret #3: Mind Your Own Business

*Make it your aim to live a quiet life, to mind your own business, and to earn your own living, just as we told you before. In this way you will win the respect of those who are not believers, and you will not have to depend on anyone for what you need".*[13]

This passage of scripture reveals some incredible life altering ideas. Firstly, it encourages us to make it our aim to live a focused life, then making sure we earn our own living. Earning our own living and minding our own business has nothing to do with having a traditional business of our own. Being focused on our own business is a mindset, not that all of us should own a business, although all of us are in business. What Paul is saying here is that even if we are an employee working for someone, or for a

---

[13] 1 Thessalonians 4:11-13

company or the government, we are in business. Our life is our business. We need to look at our life the same way a business owner looks at the company he or she runs.

It is difficult for most people to realise that even if they work for someone in a company, or for the government, they are in business. Their employer is their customer. If they changed the way they looked at themselves and their employer, their whole outlook on their job would change. Their job would not become an end in itself, but a means to an end.

Looking at ourselves as business people helps us to look at what we do from a totally different perspective. Don't look at a job, if we are an employee of that job but see it as a vehicle we use to service our client. Our client is at t our employer. Our service to our employer allows us to earn money we use to create a life we want. Our employer becomes a client, not a boss running our life. He or she becomes a means to an end, for which we are so thankful because they allow us to earn money to create the life that we want.

With this perspective, we treat our employer the same way a business person treats his or her clients. When that occurs, the employer notices and our chance of promotion is inevitable. If the employer doesn't notice, someone will, especially the other clients of our employer that we interact with. This raises our chances of earning more. And when we earn more, we raise the chances of creating a much better life for ourselves. We need to get this very clear in our minds that even if we work for someone, we are in business. We run a company called "Me Inc." and we are the CEO offering services to our employer. If we offer shoddy services to our employer, our employer will not give us more business. This is when he or she terminates the relationship. We call this getting fired, but in actual fact, it is not. This simply means that our client is not happy with our services and will definitely replace us with someone they are happy with.

Many people mourn and complain when they are fired. The same people that mourn and complain when they get laid off, also complain when they are given a shoddy service by someone. What they forget is that the service they are getting is the same they give, they are just on the other side of the counter this time. They are the client; they are in their employer's shoes.

> If we see ourselves as the CEO of our own company, providing services to our employer, our attitude changes and our chances of moving up increase.

What keeps many people stagnant in their job is that they see themselves as working for someone, instead of seeing themselves as working for themselves. If we see ourselves as the CEO of our own company, providing services to our employer, our attitude changes and our chances of moving up increase. Our employer notices that very quickly and will definitely move us up whenever he or she gets a chance.

To illustrate this point, I want to narrate a story that happened to my wife a few years back. She worked for someone for over five years but felt she wasn't growing in her career and resigned from her position of a junior manager in this company. However, during her time as a junior manager in this company, she proved that she was the best. She worked as if she owned the company. She gave it her all.

A few weeks after her resignation, she received a call from her former employer asking for a meeting. When she got to the meeting she found that her former employer was in the office with a friend. Guess what her former employer had done? After my wife resigned from his company, he took it upon himself to find her a better job. He called up a friend who had a similar business and was looking for a general manager for his business. My wife's former employer recommended her.

Why do you think someone, who leaves a company, would leave such an impact that their former employer to the extent they take it upon themselves to look for a better job for them? It is because when she was there, she didn't work as if she was merely employed. She worked as one who provided a service to her employer such that the employer still wanted the best for her, because in his company there wasn't any higher my wife would go.

I see a lot of people that dream about being successful. But when I see how they work, I am convinced no one would want to employ them if they knew how they work. There is a scripture in the gospels which says; *"He who is faithful in what is least is faithful also in much; and he who is unjust in what is least is unjust also in much. [11] Therefore if you have not been faithful in the unrighteous mammon, who will commit to your trust the true riches? [12] And if you have not been faithful in what is another man's, who will give you what is your own[14]?*

This just shows that we do not get to the next level until we outgrow the current one. Our movement up may be in the same company, organization or institution, or it could be somewhere else like it

---
[14] Luke 16: 10-12; New King James Version

happened for my wife. But going up is guaranteed if we outgrow our current position.

Therefore, secret number three is for us to mind our own business. Even if we work for someone or in an organization, we are still in business. The business of feeding our family. Of building our home. Of getting a good car and living a great life. If we work for someone or for a company or the government, we have contracted our expertise to them as a client so that we can offer a service to them to service their clients. The company or the person we work for is our client. Treat them as thus and we see that our work is not be a burden, and our outlook on the company changes. We move from being an employee to being a boss.

Treat your employer as your client and manage your financial matters as a CEO manages the financial matters of his or her own company.

Another important factor to consider from the scripture we quoted at the beginning of this chapter is that when we focus on our own business, we earn the respect of others and become self-reliant. Who doesn't want the respect that comes from handling financial matters well? We all know being financially independent is a life's desire seen in almost every normal human being.

However, because of a lack of understanding of this principle, most people don't become financially independent even after working for 30 to 40 years. Why? The reason is that they continue to work for other people. They forget something critical to financial success. Don't work for anyone, work for yourself. Treat your employer as your client and manage your financial matters as a CEO manages the financial matters of his or her own company. Don't put your lack of financial success on your employer. The employer is not your problem. You are the problem.

Can you imagine if someone came and accused you of their financial ruin? When you ask them why they think so, they say you are their client who comes to buy bread from their bakery every day when you knock off from work. This is what you are doing if you think your employer cares about your financial life.

They pay you for the service you provide. It is up to you to thank them and on your own, mind your business.

Do no not look at yourself as an employee. Look at yourself as a consultant who hired his services to help someone or a company achieve its goals while you are achieving yours. You do that by using your earnings to invest in some investment instruments, or on the stock exchange, or you can use the method that Jacob used to become self-reliant.

We must treat our financial matters as a separate entity not tied up to our work. Our work is a stream of income we use to earn money for our own financial freedom which is completely independent from our work. Our work does not determine our financial journey. Our journey is independent from our work. That is why we are not limited to having one stream of income. We are not limited to one client. We can have multiple clients as long as we provide all them with premium service.

Our financial journey is our business. That is why we are in business. The story about Jacob and

## Success Secrets from the Bible

Laban demonstrates this principle very well. Hear what Jacob told his employer Laban. *"For what you had before I came was little, and it has increased to a great amount; the LORD has blessed you [ᵃ]since my coming. And now, when shall I also provide for my own house?" **31** So he said, "What shall I give you?"And Jacob said, "You shall not give me anything. If you will do this thing for me, I will again feed and keep your flocks: **32** Let me pass through all your flock today, removing from there all the speckled and spotted sheep, and all the brown ones among the lambs, and the spotted and speckled among the goats; and these shall be my wages. **33** So my righteousness will answer for me in time to come, when the subject of my wages comes before you: every one that is not speckled and spotted among the goats, and brown among the lambs, will be considered stolen, if it is with me."**34** And Laban said, "Oh, that it were according to your word!" **35** So he removed that day the male goats that were speckled and spotted, all the female goats that were speckled and spotted, every one that had some white in it, and all the brown ones among the* *lambs, and gave them into the hand of his sons. 36 Then he put three days' journey between himself and Jacob, and Jacob fed the rest of Laban's flocks.*[15]

There are two things that we see from this story. The first is that Jacob came to a realization that financial freedom was his own business, not his employer's. Laban his boss paid him wages but what he did with that to create his freedom was up to him. This is not different from any of us. We work or run a business, but our financial freedom is our business. Working or running a business does not guarantee financial freedom if we are not focused on it, and if we don't treat it as our own business.

The second thing that we see in this passage is that Jacob didn't stop working for Laban immediately. He continued while running a separate sheep breeding business with his sons. Jacob continued working for Laban until he felt that it wasn't necessary any more. Using our employment as a source of income to create financial freedom doesn't mean we have to stop work.

---

[15] Genesis 30:30-36

We can also see he had multiple streams of income. He was getting all the speckled sheep born in Laban's flock, and his sheep also multiplied.

We can work for someone as long as we treat our financial freedom as a separate business from our job. Setting financial freedom goals is our business. Our job is a tool to earn money for our business. We are running a business and our salary is a source of income into our business.

To make this mental shift, there are principles we must subscribe to. These principles are universal and following them helps us on our journey to success. I learnt these principles reading a document from a Jewish Rabbi whose name I cannot recall, but they stuck with me ever since. Here are four timeless principles to remember if we want to mind our own business.

**Making Money is Noble**

The process of making money is despised by most people, but if we really think about it, business is what keeps the world alive today. Although we despise business, the food we eat is produced and distributed by business. All the advancements in technology that made travel safer and faster, and health care to enhance life, is all part of business. I am struggling to think of anything that makes the world a better place today that is not part of business.

Making money is just a by-product of doing business. When money is made from a legitimate business that advances and enhances life, then making money becomes a noble thing. The problem comes when people look at the money that other people have compared to the rest of world, and despise the process of making money. In most cases, people who have lots of money did it by doing something for the world that made life better. That doesn't call for our frowning. It calls for a celebration.

I will give the example of Bill Gates. He is the wealthiest person on earth. We may look at his wealth and think why should one person have all that money. Truth is, Bill Gates changed the way the world works. The personal computer changed the way we live our lives forever—for the better. He deserves all the money he has. I don't have time to mention people like Aliko Dangote of Nigeria, Strive Masiyiwa of Zimbabwe, Patrice Mustepe of South Africa, Bizos of Amazon fame. The list goes on.

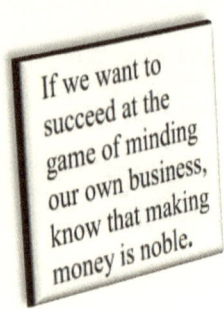

*If we want to succeed at the game of minding our own business, know that making money is noble.*

All these people have a lot of money, but when we look at what they did for humanity; they deserve every penny. The services and products they the world advanced life. Today we can travel far in a short time because of the aviation business. We have products that move fast and wide because of internet businesses like Amazon. Health care is so far advanced because now computers are able to predict certain diseases as well make surgical procedures safer. All this is due to business.

If we want to succeed at the game of minding our own business, know that making money is noble. As long as we are doing legitimate business.

Kenneth Mwale

**Dignify Your Job**

The word work is a dirty word to some people. When we look at some cultures where there is so much poverty, most people look at work as an inconvenience. Work is not an inconvenience. Work is part of who we are as humans, and it has to be dignified.

To succeed at minding our own business, we need to look at work as something dignified. We should dignify what we do so much that when we are in our place of work, we should feel like we are in a sacred place. Whatever we do that brings in an income, if it is legal and helps other humans live better, should be dignified because that is what helps us on our journey to our own financial freedom.

One of the things I appreciate in my life is having a person who helps us in the house. The value house helpers offer is so underrated. I see how both my wife and I get disoriented when the lady who helps us is away. It is almost as if our worlds are falling apart.

However, most people that do house helping work don't feel the work they do is dignified. They usually feel like they are doing something undignified.

Truth is, house helpers are doing one of the most dignified type of work. We who are able have a house helper should actually help them to feel that what they do is so dignified. We should teach our kids to respect our house helpers and we must treat them with dignity.

## Service is Worship

Believe that helping others, by adding value, is worship to God. Most people do not know that the Hebrew word 'Avodah' means both worship and service. This means every time we serve other humans we are actually worshiping God. It is not a coincidence that the same word is translated both as worship and service. Here are two places in the Bible where this word is used, but one means worship, and the other means work.

*"You shall **work (Avodah)** six days, but on the seventh day you shall rest. In plowing time and in harvest you shall rest"*[16].

*"And Jehovah spoke to Moses, Go to Pharaoh, and say to him: Thus says Jehovah, Let my people go*

---

[16] Exodus 34:21

*so that they may serve Me"*[17].

These are just two passages among many where we see the word for work and worship is the same word in Hebrew. To God, work, or service is a part of worship.

### Self-reliance is Honourable

There is no such thing as a dignified beggar. Self-reliance is the highest honor for humans. When a person lives a life of self-reliance, being able to look after themselves and their loved ones, there is a lot of honor in that.

In most cases, we don't help people because we respect them. We do so because we feel pity on them. A person who is living in poverty, is not able to take care of himself is not dignified. On the other hand, a person who earns their own living, and is self-reliant, has much to respect in that.

That is why the highest level of giving is not the giving of alms. I know most people revere the giving of alms, and handouts to the poor. That is why

---

[17] Exodus 8:1

people like Mother Teresa are heroes, because they helped the poor. Good as such deeds may be, they are not the highest form of giving.

The highest form of giving is when we help someone become self-reliant. When we empower someone, not with a handout, but with either a process or a connection or anything that sets them up to live better on their own.

Why do you think helping someone to look after themselves is better than to give them a handout? The reason is simple. When we give the person a handout, we do so out of pity. When we help someone get set up to look after themselves, we do so out of respect for human dignity.

There are times when we need to give handouts, but that should be a temporary measure. We need to celebrate people who empower others, like business men and women, more than we celebrate those who go out begging for donations. If we celebrate business, we have more dignity than when we celebrate donations.

Therefore, in light of all the things said in this

chapter, secret number three is, "Mind your own business". Even if we don't run our own business, we are in business for ourselves. Look at our financial freedom as a separate journey from our work journey. Our job is a source of income for our own financial journey. Look at making money as something noble and dignified, because it is a form of worship to God and brings self-reliance which is the highest honor for humans.

## Chapter 4

## Success Secret #4: Be Curious

*"Now Moses was tending the flock of Jethro his father-in-law, the priest of Midian. And he led the flock to the back of the desert, and came to Horeb, the mountain of God. ² And the Angel of the LORD appeared to him in a flame of fire from the midst of a bush. So he looked, and behold, the bush was burning with fire, but the bush was not consumed. ³ Then Moses said, "I will now turn aside and see this great sight, why the bush does not burn."*

*⁴ So when the LORD saw that he turned aside to look, God called to him from the midst of the bush and said, Moses, Moses!"*[18]

The story of Moses and the burning bush is one of the most told stories in the Bible. There are very few people on the planet who haven't heard this story. However, when telling the story, most people emphasize the fact that the bush was burning but

---

[18] Exodus 3:1-4

wasn't being consumed. I get that. That is one of the dramatic things that happens in this story. No wonder it catches the attention of most readers and tellers of the story. However, I think it is not the main point of the story. Why do I think so? I think so because I am very sure that not only Moses saw this burning bush that was not being consumed. There were many shepherds in that part of the mountain on that particular day who may also have seen the burning bush.

There is a line that most people miss which is so crucial to what is happening in the story.

Before I show you the line that I feel is the most crucial in this story, I want to first get back to the point I made earlier that the burning bush that wasn't being consumed was seen by many people that day. Why do I think so?

Do you remember that when Moses first appeared on the scene in this part of the world, he rescued the girls at a well, one of whom would end up being his wife? Then there were shepherds who were stopping Jethro's daughters from watering their sheep. Moses, a fugitive from Egypt at the time, appeared on the scene and became a hero to Jethro's daughters because he rescued them from those unruly shepherds. They took him to their father and Jethro gave Moses Zipporah, one of his daughters for a wife.

*"Now the priest of Midian had seven daughters. And they came and drew water, and they filled the troughs to water their father's flock. 17 Then the shepherds came and drove them away; but Moses stood up and helped them, and watered their flock. 18 When they came to Reuel[] their father, he said, "How is it that you have come so soon today?" 19 And they said, "An Egyptian delivered us from the hand of the shepherds, and he also drew enough water for us and watered the flock." 20 So he said to his daughters, "And where is he? Why is it that you have left the man? Call him, that he may eat bread." 21 Then Moses was content to live with the man, and he gave Zipporah his daughter to Moses.*

That is proof that that Moses was not the only one that day who saw that bush burning and not getting consumed. Why then was it a big deal to Moses?

In Exodus 3:4, the Bibles says, *"And when the LORD **saw that he turned aside to see**, God called* *unto him out of the midst of the bush"*. God didn't call Moses because Moses was a good shepherd, different from the others. No. According to verse 4, God called Moses because Moses was the only one that

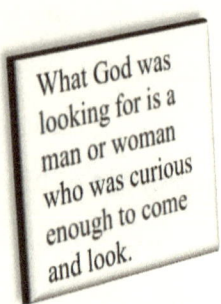

day that turned aside to look at the bush that was burning and not getting consumed. That is the central point in this story not the miracle of the bush not getting consumed by fire.

What God was looking for is a man or woman who was curious enough to come and look. He could have used any method to attract attention. The method is inconsequential; it was curiosity He was looking for. Some people have also said that burning bushes were a common phenomenon in the desert because of high heat levels. Whatever the case, God used that to see who was going to be inquisitive and come closer to look.

Curiosity is one of the success secrets from the Bible. A person who is curious always attracts a call to something, more so than one who goes through life without any sense of wonder. Those who always look for things that make them wonder end up discovering new ways of doing things. In so doing, they end up becoming inventors or founders of great companies. Only the curious discover new things. It is the new things that bring about new business and new organisations etc.

When we study the history of science and technology, we see that people like Sir Isaac Newton, the guy who discovered gravity, were curious people. While fruits fell from trees every day, Isaac Newton wanted to find out what drew the fruit to the ground. Why would the fruit not just float in the air when it disconnected from the tree? Because of this, he ended up discovering gravity, a phenomenon that we are harnessing today to do many things including world travel. If he wasn't inquisitive enough, we wouldn't know about the pull of gravity.

Every invention and technology comes from people like sir Isaac Newton who are curious. They spend hours and hours observing things to find out why those things behave the way they do and they use that knowledge to invent things to help people.

In 1945, a man named Percy Spencer was doing his normal duties at a company called Raytheon, when the candy he was carrying in his pocket melted. Curious why the candy melted without normal heat, he ended up discovering the technology that we use in microwave ovens today. I am sure this phenomenon happened to other people in his company because Raytheon was a company that developed microwave radar transmitters during World War II[19]. Why did others in his company not invent the Microwave oven? The answer is simple; they weren't curious enough to ask why did things melt without heat?

To succeed in life, we need to have a mind that is curious. Ask questions. Have a mind that wants to learn more, know more, and do more. Don't be satisfied with the status quo. Try to go beyond the obvious and see more than what everyone else sees.

---

[19] https://wonderopolis.org/wonder/who-invented-the-microwave-oven

## Kenneth Mwale

Opportunities are everywhere looking for people with a curious mind.

Curiosity attracts opportunities. There are so many opportunities to start new businesses and new organizations in the world today. However, because people's curiosity is low, we aren't getting more and more people starting new things and discovering new things. All that we see today are mega companies providing services in the tech field which were started by curious people—people who saw an opportunity where everyone else saw nothing. Or is it that they wanted to see more than what everybody saw? They went beyond the obvious. Like Moses, Spencer and Isaac Newton, they wanted to know more about something that everyone else probably took for granted.

Opportunities are everywhere looking for people with a curious mind. It was Helen Keller who said, "The only thing worse than being blind is having sight without vision". Everyone who has eyes can look, but only those that are curious can see. To see is different from looking. Looking has to do with receiving an image into our brain to learn facts about what is going on. To see goes beyond looking, in that it asks questions about what we are looking at.

Two people can look at the same thing but see two totally different things. What separates those who will end up succeeding and those that won't is what they see. Successful people see what others don't see. While everybody complains about something, a curious person sees a business opportunity. While everybody complains about this and that, a curious person is busy asking questions of how he or she can harness that and create a business.

The Bible in the book of Ecclesiastes gives a clue as to what curiosity is. *"The wise man's eyes are in his head, But the fool walks in darkness. Yet I myself perceived That the same event happens to them all"*.[20]

A story is told about two shoe salesmen. The first one was sent to a village to sell shoes and came back with a complaint to his superiors that it was impossible to sell shoes in that particular village because no one

---

[20] Ecclesiastes 2:14

wore shoes. The second salesperson was sent to the same village and came back so motivated about the vastness of the market because there was not a single person in the village that wore shoes.

This story, which I don't know if is a true story or not, is a typical example of curiosity. The first salesperson complained about the same situation that made the friend motivated. This is what separates those who end up succeeding and those who end up poor for the rest of their lives. One saw a market, but the other man saw only why he wasn't going to succeed.

Success secret number four is curiosity. Don't just look at things. See what you are looking at. Have eyes inside your head, not only on your forehead. Ask relevant questions, don't just complain.

Success Secrets from the Bible

## Chapter 5

## Success Secret #5; Know What You Bring to the Deal

*"Laban said to him, "Let me say this: I have learned by divination that the LORD has blessed me because of you"*[21].

Isn't it ironic that Laban said to Jacob that God had blessed him because of Jacob? Why would God bless Laban not Jacob if the blessing was because of Jacob? We see the same pattern repeating itself in one of Jacob's sons Joseph. Potiphar his master also said the same thing that he had perceived that God had blessed him, Potiphar, because of Joseph.

*"So it was, from the time that he had made him overseer of his house and all that he had, that the LORD blessed the Egyptian's house for*

---

[21] Genesis 30:25; New King James Version

*Joseph's sake; and the blessing of the* LORD *was on all that he had in the house and in the field"*[22].

I have always wondered why God would bless someone on because of someone else. Why not just send the blessing to the person who is blessed? In the New Testament, there is a sad story that gives light as to why God sometimes does this Matthew 25. A master gave his workers some capital but one of them chose not to put it to work to multiply it. When you choose not to use what you have, someone may do and what was even meant to be yours become theirs and they choose how much of what they have produced should be given to you.

*"So take the talent from him, and give it to him who has ten talents.* [29] *'For to everyone who has, more will be given, and he will have abundance; but from him who does not have, even what he has will be taken away"*[23].

In this story, someone didn't use their talent and God decided to take from them the little they have to give to someone who had more. While this

---

[22] Genesis 39:5; New King James Version
[23] Matthew 25:28-29; New King James Version

arrangement looks unfair to the person who had a little, and in the two other stories in Genesis. The truth is that if you don't understand your value, the blessing will always go to the person who does and they are the one who will give you what they think you are worth. You become a channel of the blessing but you don't get to decide about your own blessing. That is why it is not enough to just be blessed, you also need wisdom.

These stories help us to understand the importance of understanding the value we bring to a transaction. Many people are so ignorant of what value they bring to the transaction so much so that they have to be told what value they bring and most of times because the people on the other side of table want maximum return, unless they are ethical, they will always under state the value you bring.

In every transactional relationship, know what you are bringing to the transaction, and what the other person is bringing. A value transaction is different from any other relationship. It is different in that its fairness is dependent on an exchange of value, but that value is between the two who are exchanging the value. Most people transact without understanding what they bring and later on cry. We will look at that in depth when we look at the transaction of Esau and Jacob.

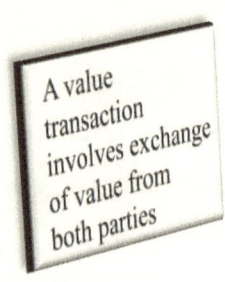

A value transaction involves exchange of value from both parties

A value transaction involves exchange of value from both parties. The aim is not to get more than you are putting in, but to get the worth of what you are putting in. Always aim for a win win transaction whenever a value transaction is being negotiated. Don't try to outsmart the other person, but also don't allow them to outsmart you. The Bible is very clear about this; *"Dishonest[a] scales are an abomination to the LORD, But a [b]just weight is His delight"*[24].

There is no place in the Bible where this is best explained than in the story of Jacob and his brother Esau as told in Genesis 25.

*"Now Jacob cooked a stew; and Esau came in from the field, and he was weary. 30 And Esau said to Jacob, "Please feed me with that same red stew, for*

---

[24] Proverbs 11:1; New King James Version

*I am weary." Therefore his name was called [ᵍ]Edom. But Jacob said, "Sell me your birthright as of this day." **32** And Esau said, "Look, I am about to die; so what is this birthright to me?" **33** Then Jacob said, [ʰ] "Swear to me as of this day." So he swore to him, and sold his birthright to Jacob. **34** And Jacob gave Esau bread and stew of lentils; then he ate and drank, arose, and went his way. Thus Esau despised his birthright"*²⁵.

> Esau came to transact with his brother Jacob but was very oblivious about the value he was bringing to the transaction.

Jacob who we see in the opening scripture being a victim of a lopsided value transaction, had earlier in his childhood done the same to his brother Esau. It is as if God is helping him to understand that you reap what you saw. Nonetheless, that is a lesson for another day. Now we are discussing the importance of knowing the value you are bring to a transaction.

Esau came to transact with his brother Jacob but was very oblivious about the value he was bringing

---

²⁵ Genesis 25:29-34; New King James version

to the transaction. Being a first born in this culture had a lot of future value implications but he decided either not to take advantage of that or was too occupied with his hunger that it blinded him to the real value he was bringing to the table. Jacob on the other hand was very clear about what he wanted in exchanged for his stew. On the other hand, Esau took what he had for granted and in the end he got a raw deal.

Many people have accused Jacob of stealing the birthright from his brother. While yes he was not fair in the price he asked for his stew, Esau had all the time in the world to negotiate a better deal. Jacob just put the price on the table, it was up to him to either refuse or put his own on the table as well. At least if he asked for a supply of stew for a lifetime it was going to make sense. It again for Jacob to refuse or take. That is what value transactions look like, you have to negotiate until you get what you feel is fair.

Never get into any transaction that you don't understand how much value you will add. It is what value you add that determines what you are justifiably supposed to ask back. Like earlier said, the aim is not to get more, but to get out of a transaction what is justifiably fair to you and the other person.

What I have observed is that most people struggle with the idea of putting value on their transaction. I see this a lot in job interviews. Most people can confidently answer all technical questions in a job interview until they asked how much they think is a fair salary for the work they will be doing? "So, how much money do you think we should pay you for this position?" The interviewer would ask. At this point they look down, and start fidgeting with their phone, or with their hands, and some have even point blankly said, "I am not here for the money". This is not true because if they were not there for the money, why did they apply for the job? The problem is that they cannot put a value on the transaction, not because they are not in it for the money, but they don't understand.

If you are not in it for the money, then don't do a money transaction. Come in as pro-bono right up front. Most relationships are ruined with people who do not understand value because either they expect too much for too little contribution, or they come without a specific expectation and when they are given what the "Laban" thinks they are worth, they go out despondent and start to complain. Sometimes it just happens that after they have received an offer, they discover someone who got more out of the same value they provided. At this point they cry as if it is the other person's problem. Just like Esau did, they don't negotiate and cry later. The best is to negotiate first to avoid crying later.

The best way of dealing with a value transactional relationship is to put things on the table and clearly state one's expectations. If the expectations cannot be met, then you greet and part ways without any broken relationships. The problem comes when you enter a value transactional relationship with unclear expectations. When that happens, just know that in the end someone will get hurt.

Here are a few things to consider from the story of Jacob and his brother Esau that will help you deal with value transactions.

Kenneth Mwale

**1. Don't negotiate when you are hungry**

This has got nothing to do with actual hunger, it's got everything to do with attitude of desperation. Most people come into a value transaction from a point of desperation. Every time you are in a desperate state, don't make financial decisions. Make sure even if your situation is dire, prepare your mind to operate as if all was well.

When you are in a desperate state of mind, you only see now, you don't see tomorrow. Your friend who may be in a better position may see things different and will bring their right value on the table but because you are desperate, you will sell yourself short.

When you go for an interview for example. Even if you haven't been employed for many years, don't go as if your life depends on the job, even if it may. Wash yourself, if you have to borrow perfume do so, so that you can smell a million bucks when you walk in. People usually have the mistaken idea that when you look desperate people will feel sorry for you and give you a job. People don't do business with desperate people, and they don't give jobs to desperate people. If you want a hand out, then it is a good thing to look desperate. But if you want a real solution, act the part and look and smell the part.

If you want a handout, play desperate. If you want to score a business deal, or get a job, show up looking like you have the solution. If you show up looking like you need help, you may get help in form of a loaf of bread, but not a job or a business deal in the bag.

**2. Always look at the intangibles**

The intangibles are those things that seem inconsequential during your desperate moment. For example, most people think self-respect is inconsequential when they are desperate. While it may seem so, the truth is that it only seems so because you are desperate. Self-respect is everything, and you have to maintain it even if you have no food at home. Don't let your dignity fall to the floor just because you need help. Be yourself. Be together and act as if you are an honorable person even when you have nothing, because at all times, the intangibles remain intact.

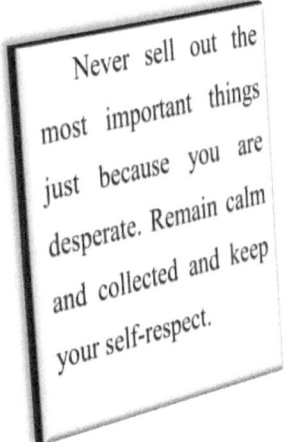

Even if Esau was hungry and his birthright seemed like nothing, His birthright is an intangible so it wasn't affected by hunger. It is him who thought so, but it was still intact and he through it in the mud. His birthright was an intangible thing that is not affected by something physical. He was a hungry first born. His state of first born remained intact no matter how hungry he got.

Never sell out the most important things just because you are desperate. Remain calm and collected and keep your self-respect.

### 3. Look at the future value not present realities

I usually say that people are usually stuck on what they see not what they can be. When they look at what they are today, they do things that they come to regret in future because they do not look at what can be, but what is.

A man or woman who sells himself or herself shot of their dignity comes to regret one day when one moment of pleasure stands in her way of political office. They realize that what they did a long time ago, at the time when they thought they are a nobody, now stands in the way of them becoming a somebody. Truth is that even then they were still a somebody but they didn't know that because that only promised future value.

There are certain things that may look like they have no value today in your life. The same thing tomorrow may be the thing that either take you up or bring you down. Like those intangibles, remember, something may look like it has no value today. Tomorrow that may be the most valuable thing in your life.

4. **Value is in the transaction not in what is being transacted.**

## Kenneth Mwale

One of the things I had to learn the hard way was to realize that value is in the transaction and not what is being transacted. What this means is that value is dynamic in every transaction and it is the two or more people that are involved in a transaction that should negotiate what each brings to the transactions, and what that is worth. If that is not done up front, you can be sure someone in the end will cry foul and bad things are bound to happen.

In the story of Jacob and Esau, Esau was the one who didn't know the value of what he was bringing to the transaction. After the transaction was sealed, Esau accused Jacob of stealing from him. The truth is that Jacob stole nothing. Esau put a value on his birthright. Jacob had stew and he said his stew was worth a birthright. Esau said he had a birthright and it was worth a plate of stew. Transaction done!!! There was no reason for Esau to come back and say Jacob was a thief. If there was anyone who was a thief, it was Esau because in the end he still wanted to remain the first born and get the first born blessing. Truth is that a few years prior to that day when Isaac wanted to bless him as the first born, he should have told his father that no dad, I am now the second born. I sold my birthright to Jacob.

# Chapter 6

## Success Secret #6: Action Precedes Learning

*"Then the Lord said to Moses, "Why are you crying out to me? Tell the Israelites to move on. ⁱ⁶ Raise your staff and stretch out your hand over the sea to divide the water so that the Israelites can go through the sea on dry ground"* [26]

There was a time in the field of business when people wrote a hundred-page business plan to present to a bank for funding. The bank judged whether the plan would become a profitable business based on how good the plan was written not with reality check in the real market. Depending on the bank's judgement, the business plan either attracted funding or received a no funding response.

---

[26] Exodus 14:15-16

## Success Secrets from the Bible

The world of business has evolved a lot in the past few years, especially since the advent of the internet. Most multi-billion dollar businesses today never had a business plan. Most businesses like Google, Yahoo, and other tech giants received funding without a hundred-page business plan. Most did not have a written plan, but only a good idea told to Venture Capitalist and boom, money was given, and today we have these big companies.

Most of these companies received funding because someone saw the idea and believed in the power of the idea. However, the people behind the idea had a lot to do with the success of these companies.

Ideas come to all of us. It is what we do with them that makes a difference. However, what we do with the ideas that come to us depends on the type of person the idea comes from. Two people can have the same idea, one becomes a multi-billionaire from the idea, while another person languishes with poverty with the same idea.

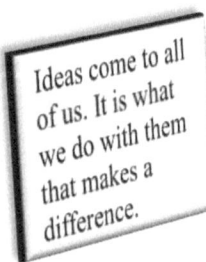
Ideas come to all of us. It is what we do with them that makes a difference.

The problem is not the idea. The problem is how the idea becomes a business. There are processes that an idea should go through if it will see the light of day. Some of these processes kill a good idea, while others give the idea a fair chance of surviving to become a great business.

Therefore, what processes make ideas flourish to become great businesses? To answer this question, I want to introduce you to an idea that was popularised by a guy called Eric Ries.

**The Lean Start Up Method**

I stumbled upon this idea a few years ago in a book called the *Lean Start Up*. The idea postulated in this book is quite revolutionary. He shows a method which makes a business plan such an archaic idea.

The whole idea behind the lean start up method is to test a business idea on the market, and learn from how the market responds to the idea. While a business plan remains on paper with all the theorising of what could or can be. The lean start-up method says whatever we want to do, take it to the actual market in small doses and see how the market responds. As we test the market, keep all the data that we get from how the market is responding to help us to make adjustments to the product or services.

I think this way of starting a business has a more realistic chance of creating an accurate response than a guy who sits in a bank somewhere telling us whether our business will work or not. There are so many businesses that could have become multi-billion dollar businesses if the people possessing the ideas used the lean start up method rather than going to the bank to ask someone who may not know anything about the business we want to start.

One of the most popular business reality shows is the *Dragon's Den*. Again, this program is about people sharing business ideas in front of a panel to woo one of the panellists to invest in their idea. No lengthy business plans. Just a presentation and guts.

Now, why am I saying all this you may ask? I am saying all this because of success secret number six. This success secret from the bible is very much in line with the above business start-up method. I actually believe that the right way of putting it is that the lean starts up method is in line with the biblical secret number six. This secret has been used longer than the lean start-up by Jewish people.

Secret number six states that we have to do first and learn later from actual data from our interaction with the market.

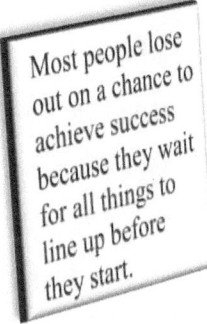

When Moses cried out to the Lord in front of the Red Sea, God told him to tell the children of Israel to march forward. After he told them to march forward, then God said to him, now stretch forth your rod over the sea. The sequence of events is such that Moses told people to move first and that is when he stretched forth his rod. He didn't stretch the rod and then the people move forward.

Rabbi Daniel Lapin teaches in his ancient Jewish wisdom series that the sea didn't part until some of the people where neck deep in the water. There are things that don't move until we move. There are certain lessons we cannot learn until we test them. Someone once said that we cannot know how far we can fly until we actually fly. There is no testing for flying that can tell us how far we can go if we don't actually do it.

I want to believe that even if what Rabbi Lapin is suggesting is not shown in the text. I agree with the Rabbi because a similar incident happened when they were crossing the River Jordan. God told Joshua to ask the Levites carrying the Ark of the Covenant to "step into the water for the water to part"[27]. The Bible says as soon as they put their feet in the water, the water parted. If the Levites waited for the water to part without first stepping in it, the water wouldn't have parted.

Most people lose out on a chance to achieve success because they wait for all things to line up before they start. Sometimes starting is all there is to success because like they say, "success breeds success". There are a lot of things that until we do them, we won't know what could have been.

---

[27] Joshua 3:8; New King James Version

Another important lesson about this is that classroom education is so overrated. I think most of the things we end up doing in life, we don't learn in class. We learn them when we put our hands to the plough.

We can also learn something from the Bible in Deuteronomy 15:10. This is what it says: *"You shall surely give to him, and your heart should not be grieved when you give to him, because for this thing the LORD your God will bless you in all your works and in all to which you put your hand"*. Sometimes we stifle our own growth and hinder our blessings because we wait. We don't need to wait. We need to be on the move and as we go, we will learn what works and what doesn't.

To wait for everything to line up is one of the biggest lies about how life works. We learn as we go. We get better as we practice. We shouldn't allow ourselves to get into what has been called analysis paralysis. We analyze until we become paralyzed.

Success secret number six from the Bible is "do and learn later". The more we do the more we improve.

The reason we improve is because key information is acquired when we do.

## Chapter 7

## Success Secret #7: Man cannot live on bread alone

*"Jesus answered, "It is written: 'Man shall not live on bread alone, but on every word that comes from the mouth of God."*[28]

*"David said to the Philistine, "You come against me with sword and spear and javelin, but I come against you in the name of the* LORD *Almighty, the God of the armies of Israel, whom you have defied.* [46] *This day the* LORD *will deliver you into my hands, and I'll strike you down and cut off your head. This very day I will give the carcasses of the Philistine army to the birds and the wild animals, and the whole world will know that there is a God in Israel.* [47] *All those gathered here will know that it is not by sword or spear that the* LORD *saves; for the battle is the* LORD*'s, and he will give all of you into our hands."*[29]

---

[28] Matthew 4:4 NIV
[29] 1 Samuel 17:45-477

The story of David and Goliath is one of the most popular Sunday school stories. While I like the fact this story has become so popular within Christendom, I still feel most of the lessons in the story are either miscommunicated, or blatantly given wrong meaning.

The first misconception in the story is they say David was a little inexperienced boy. While it is true he was a boy, it is not true he was inexperienced. Saul told David he was inexperienced, but David rebuffed his statement by telling him that he killed both a lion and a bear during his time as a shepherd. He went on to say because of that, he was well able to fight the Philistine. Talk about experience. I don't think an inexperienced person could kill a lion or a bear.

David also refused to wear the armor given to him by Saul, because he said he was not experienced with that type of armor. He chose the weapon he was experienced in. David was an experience sling thrower. He hit Goliath's forehead not as a fluke, but because he aimed at it.

Another misconception of the story is about the stones. Most people I have heard "spiritualize" the stones. They say because he took five stones, each stone stands for a letter in the word GRACE. This is not true either because the Old Testament was not written in English, and the word grace is not five letters in every language.

The story of David and Goliath, especially the statement that, *"You come against me with sword and spear and javelin, but I come against you in the name of the LORD Almighty, the God of the armies of Israel, whom you have defied"*[30] gives an impression that killing Goliath didn't require a physical weapon. Other people trivialize the use of the sling and stone. They say that David did not have to aim at Goliath because the Holy Spirit directed the stone. This is not true either. David was an experienced sling thrower, and God used him for that reason. God was with the Children of Israel on that battle field, but no one killed Goliath before David came.

---

[30] 1 Samuel 18:45 NIV

When David said, "I come to you in the name of Lord", he also said, "God does not deliver with sword and shield". But he ended up going down to the river to take five stones to throw at Goliath. Why use stones if God didn't require a weapon to kill Goliath? Again, why take five stones and not just one?

There are a few things critical to our success in this story. The first is that working with God does not mean removing ourselves from the equation. Working with God is to marry the physical and the spiritual together as a unit.

Secondly, David didn't take one stone. We already dealt with the misconception of the stones. Truth is, t David gave himself five chances to throw the stone. He knew his level of competence was one out of five. He wasn't going to miss five times. There was no need for David to get five stones if, as people say, The Holy Spirit directed the stones

Thirdly, David used what he was experienced in. He refused the spear and shield and said that God does not deliver with "ONLY" the spear and shield. He used a weapon familiar to him, the sling and a stone.

What I think is at that time maybe no one thought of using this weapon. Another lesson to learn. Don't be stuck in your ways, God may ask you to do something out of the norm.

## Sacred and Secular

The danger of removing ourselves from the equation when it comes to "God" is doing something which creates a wrong way of looking at life. We tend to look at certain aspects of our lives as sacred and others as secular. The secular is despised and the sacred revered. This is a wrong paradigm to live by.

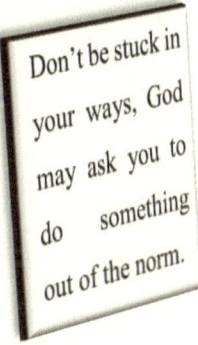

I don't look at life as secular and sacred. I look at it as a unit of spiritual and physical. It is a fusion of two making one. Not a sum of the two, but a unit. To succeed one needs to bring these two worlds into one.

## The Battle of Amalek

*"The Amalekites came and attacked the Israelites at Rephidim. $^9$ Moses said to Joshua, "Choose some of our men and go out to fight the Amalekites. Tomorrow I will stand on top of the hill with the staff of God in my hands." $^{10}$ So Joshua fought the Amalekites as Moses had ordered, and Moses, Aaron and Hur went to the top of the hill. $^{11}$ As long as Moses held up his hands, the Israelites were winning, but whenever he lowered his hands, the Amalekites were winning. $^{12}$ When Moses' hands grew tired, they took a stone and put it under him and he sat on it. Aaron and Hur held his hands up—one on one side, one on the other—so that his hands remained steady till sunset. $^{13}$ So Joshua overcame the Amalekite army with the sword".*[31]

To help us understand the power of bringing these two together. The Bible again provides a great example in the Battle of Amalek. The passage of scripture I quoted above is commonly used to illustrate the need for leaders to have support from those they

---

[31] Exodus 17:8-19 NIV

lead. I have no problem with that perspective at all. There is truth in that. Actually, scripture a form of literature that usually has multiple meanings to one story. One passage can mean a dozen other things, and each is correct.

I don't refute the fact that this passage can be used to illustrate the need for support, but my perspective is quite different. In the drama that unfolds on top of the mountain, and the battle being waged in the valley, I see the power that is in the marriage of the spiritual and physical.

When we let the spiritual and physical work in partnership, great things happen. Moses prayed to God with His hand raised over the battle field, but Joshua needed to physically fight the Amalekites. In verse 19, we see that the Bible says Amalek was defeated by the sword. While that is true, we also see *"As long as Moses held up his hands, the Israelites were winning, but whenever he lowered his hands, the Amalekites were winning*[32]. So who won the battle? Was it Moses or Joshua. I say both.

---

[32] Exodus 17:11 NIV

Success Secrets from the Bible

The two worked hand in hand. We can't say that prayer won the battle nor can we say that Joshua didn't need prayer. We usually elevate one over the other when we compartmentalise the two. 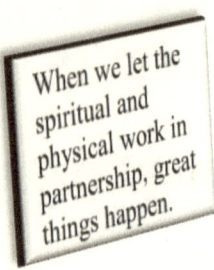 These two actions should always work together. There is no need for us to look at one as more important than the other.

God in His wisdom, created us as a combination, having a spiritual and material side. These two are not a sum of each other but they make one life. There are those who elevate the spiritual side of things and separate themselves into secluded places to get in touch with their spiritual side, so they say. They look at the spirit side of who we are as the most important, and look down on physical things. They elevate a life of solitude and sometimes even look down on material wealth and say those things have no eternal value. Yes, they may not have eternal value, but have value for our lives now. We are not yet in heaven.

## Kenneth Mwale

I tend to hold a different view. I look at life as a unit of spirit and physical matter. I don't see where one ends and another starts. I see one whole made up of spirit and physical. When I want to make a decision, I pray and assess the situation physically. I use both my spiritual faculties and my physical endowments and every time that combination is in good tension, I tend to make the right decision.

To succeed in life one needs to have a very good tension of the two. Even the Lord Jesus Himself said we need to "watch and pray"[33]. We need to do both. Not only one.

Most people think that a miracle is what happens when they are not involved physically. There are those who want God to help them achieve success so they pray and sit. They think that God will create a tsunami of money and bring it into their lap. What they need to do is to pray and go do something. God says "He directs the steps of the righteous."[34] That should

---

[33] Matthew 26:41 NIV
[34] Psalms 37:23

tell us that there is movement from our side as well. He cannot direct the feet that are still.

Then again there are those who think because we cannot measure spiritual things, they are not real. They don't believe there is more to life than what they see. They don't believe in the spiritual side of things. Such people believe in action without consulting God. To them what cannot be measured is not real.

Both those who elevate the spiritual above the physical, and those who elevate the physical above the spiritual are wrong. Life is made up of both. Both are equally important and must be given the right place. Joshua needed to be on the battle field, but so did Moses need to be on top of the mountain praying for the battle to be won. We can't say Moses played a more important role than Joshua. Neither can we say Joshua is the one who won the battle. Both prayer and the sword won the battle.

Therefore, secret number seven is that we must marry the physical and the spiritual. These two make up what life is all about. We need to live with a good tension of both, because both are important.

## Chapter 8

### Success Secret #8: You are a Hebrew

*"A man who had escaped came and reported this to Abram the Hebrew"[35].*

The word Hebrew means "One who crosses over". Especially crossing over a body of water like a river or a sea. Abraham and his descendants were called Hebrews because they crossed the Euphrates river to settle in the land God showed them.

Figuratively speaking, a Hebrew is someone who is able to transform themselves by overcoming an obstacle, or obstacles. Life poses many obstacles on the way to success and only those who are willing to overcome what they find along the way to success are able to succeed. There is not a single person I know who succeeded without obstacles. If that was the case, all of us would be successful.

---

[35] Genesis 14:13: NIV

As "spiritual" Hebrews, all God's children are supposed to crossover whatever obstacle stands in their way to God's destiny. Obstacles are not there to stop us. They are there to reveal our character and God's power. Those who don't cross over don't do so because they lack the ability to cross. They do so because they don't live out their Hebraic identity.

Human beings are the only one of God's creations that are able to transform themselves. We may not have chosen the circumstances in which we were born, but to remain in them is our choice. God blessed every human with the potential to change their circumstances.

Who we are today is not all that we are.

Like Abraham the Hebrew, to succeed, someone should leave their negative past and pursue a future completely disassociated with their past. They should look at themselves as a completely different person. Who we are today is not all that we are. We are not condemned to stay in the circumstances that we are in right now. God hasn't locked our destiny into whatever circumstances we are in. If we feel locked up or condemned to be what we are today, it means we have created our own prison. Our prison is not real; it is a figment of our imagination.

In Chapter 12 of Genesis, the scriptures tell us what Abraham left behind.

*"Now the LORD had said to Abram: "Get out of your country, From your family And from your father's house, To a land that I will show you. 2 I will make you a great nation; I will bless you And make your name great; And you shall be a blessing"*[36].

In this passage lies a secret of what we need to leave behind if we want to succeed. These things usually hold us back on our way to success. I would like to list them below and elaborate each one.

### 1. Leave your Country and your Relatives

The reason Abram was called a Hebrew, is because he left his country and his relatives to cross over the Euphrates River. The act of leaving a country

---

[36] Genesis 12:1-2

and relatives is a show of character to leave what is familiar.

We all grow up in certain environments where we become conditioned to certain ways of thinking. We grow up in families where we adopt certain beliefs about ourselves and life in general. Most of the time the things we adopt stand in our way to God's destiny. Our duty is to challenge every negative belief about who we are and about life that our country and relatives downloaded into our subconscious. By challenging our belief system and believing in new things is like leaving a country, and leaving our relatives to go to live in a different country. Even if we do not physically leave, the fact that we don't embrace the common wrong beliefs and do not live out the wrong beliefs is like leaving a country and our relatives.

**Soil/Land - Your Success Code**

When Adam sinned, God said that out of the sweat of his brow he was going to eat. He also said that from soil he was taken and from soil he will go. But we also see that God used soil to create man and breathed his breath in him for him to become a living soul. Soil and man have a lot of figurative similarities. That holds a secret about success that most people miss.

Soil, or earth, is very significant to our success because the same potential that soil has to hold civilisation, man also has to change his or her life. When we look at everything that we use, it probably came from soil. The success code is in understanding the way soil works.

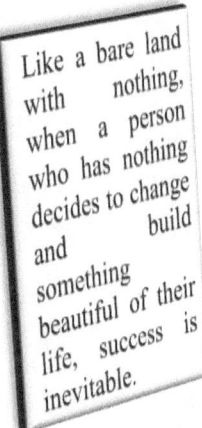

Like a bare land with nothing, when a person who has nothing decides to change and build something beautiful of their life, success is inevitable.

While the soil does not do much, it is in soil that things grow, and it is on soil that all civilisation is built, and from it that things are mined. The potential of soil is that today it maybe a bare land, and tomorrow a beautiful house, or city, is exactly the same with us as humans. Today, we may meet someone that really doesn't look like anybody, tomorrow we will be shocked that the same person has completely changed.

Success Secrets from the Bible

The first man was called Adam because he was taken from soil. Adamah, the Hebrew word used for soil is connected to Adam's name. The reason is because in Adam, like in the soil, is limitless potential to change. When we see Adam today, he may not look much, or have much, but don't be fooled, if we come tomorrow things can be different

When Adam, or man decides to crossover, things change. Like a bare land with nothing, when a person who has nothing decides to change and build something beautiful of their life, success is inevitable.

What stops us from succeeding is not the obstacle in our way, but our belief that we haven't got the ability to overcome the obstacle. Like a bare land, we see the bare land not the potential it possesses to host something beautiful.

### What is Man?

*"what are human beings, that you think of them; mere mortals, that you care for them?* [5] *Yet you*

*made them inferior only to yourself;[b] you crowned them with glory and honor"*[37]

Man is the crown of God's creation. The Bible says man is only inferior to God. This is very big statement. To know this is to become liberated from all which hinders man from succeeding and doing the work God put him here for.

God crowned man with glory. Glory is not in the undeveloped potential. While all humans have same worth in the sight of the Lord. The glory in man is only seen when man decides to work on the potential that God put in him. When that is untapped man is like a land that is uncultivated.

### Cultivate your Garden.

*"UNUSED FIELDS could yield plenty of food for the poor, but unjust people keep them from being farmed"*[38] *"Then the Lord God placed the man in the Garden of Eden to cultivate it and guard it"*[39]

---

[37] Psalms 8:4-5
[38] Proverbs 13:23
[39] Genesis 2:9

While the soil may possess unlimited potential. That potential can only be yielded if the soil is cultivated. Even humans are like that. When a human being does not use his potential, he remains like a patch of land that is uncultivated. It is our duty to cultivate our potential. Humans are the only of God's creation that have power to change their circumstance. All other forms of creation are to change their circumstances because they are at the mercy of nature.

While animals may move and go out to look for food, if nature does not provide for food, they cannot go out to plant, or cultivate for themselves. Man is different. He is capable of overcoming seemingly impossible challenges to better his environment. This knowledge is critical for success.

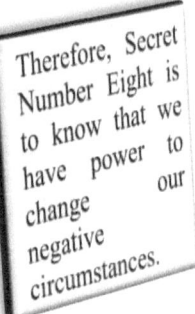

Therefore, Secret Number Eight is to know that we have power to change our negative circumstances.

In another place in the Book of Proverbs, the Lord give an explicit example of what happens to people that do not develop their potential.

## Kenneth Mwale

*"I walked through the fields and vineyards of a lazy, stupid person. [31] They were full of thorn bushes and overgrown with weeds. The stone wall around them had fallen down. [32] I looked at this, thought about it, and learned a lesson from it: [33] Go ahead and take your nap; go ahead and sleep. Fold your hands and rest awhile, [34] but while you are asleep, poverty will attack you like an armed robber[40].*

The above scripture is a depiction of a person who decides not to work on their Hebraic identity. These are people who don't know they have power to change circumstances, but instead they decide to fold their arms and sleep. Sleeping in this case may not be the actual act of sleeping, but it signifies someone who doesn't do anything about their potential.

Therefore, Secret Number Eight is to know that we have power to change our negative circumstances. As a human, just like a land can be bare, overgrown weeds and nothing much to show for, it still has potential to be a place where great developments can

---

[40] Proverbs 24:30-34

take place. Beautiful building can be built on land that today seems to be just bare and unused.

## Chapter 9

## Success Secret #9: Aim for Retirement

*"Thus the heavens and the earth were finished, and all the host of them. And on the seventh day God ended his work which he had made; and he rested on the seventh day from all his work which he had made. And God blessed the seventh day, and sanctified it: because that in it he had rested from all his work which God created and made".*[41]

"Afterward Jesus found him in the temple, and said to him, "See, you have been made well. Sin no more, lest a worse thing come upon you." The man departed and told the Jews that it was Jesus who had made him well. For this reason the Jews persecuted Jesus, [a]and sought to kill Him, because He had done these things on the Sabbath. But Jesus answered

---

[41] Genesis 2:1-3; NIV

them, "My Father has been working until now, and I have been working."[42]

The concept of retirement is very confusing to most people. To many, it means that time when we are in our 60s and are told we are too old to work anymore. 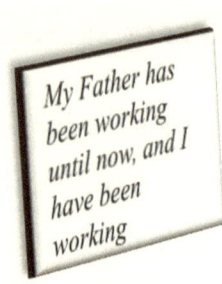 Problem with this is that it was true about 100 years ago when a person in his 60s was really old because of the type of word we did. Our industries had just been automated and most machines required manual labor. After working for 20 to 30 years for sure someone was beaten up and had to rest.

I read somewhere that a person who will leave for 150 years is already 50 years old. Can you imagine if that person retires at 65, he will have to live for 85 years doing nothing? You can see how our concepts of work did not evolve with the times.

---

[42] John 5:14-17; NIV

Another problem I see with this way of thinking is that with the advancement of health care, people will live longer and can work even in their 70s or even 80s because they are healthy. Nonetheless, while all these things can justify my point that there is no need for retirement at 65, my understanding of retirement is very different from the one that has to do with stopping work. I believe according to God; we cannot retire because we cannot stop adding value to society. On the other hand, retirement has nothing to do with stopping work.

Ordinarily, retirement is when a person is considered not fit to work because of old age. By this time, they are expected to have saved up enough money through an investment company or an insurance company to help them live through their old age. They pay a monthly amount to sustain them in their old age.

I am all for preparing for old age but I have a problem with this concept of retirement. It goes against two very important principles of how God expects us to live. The first is that we are not supposed to stop working if we are still healthy. We can change the pace, the amount of strain, or even what we do but we should not stop working. I see most people do not live long after they stop working. It looks like God created us in such a way that when we have something to do, especially a type of work that add value to our fellow humans, our lives are enriched and we live long. But when a person feels that they are not adding any value, they wilt and die.

Secondly the concept of retirement that stops people from working stops many people from enjoying life while they are still young and vibrant. Most people think of traveling and seeing the world when they retire. This is not supposed to be the way we should live. We should travel, see the world and do all that we want to do throughout our life time, not in retirement.

I subscribe to another type of retirement. Firstly, I don't believe that a human being comes to a time when their potential become exhausted and they have parked on the way side and get paid a little amount of money by the government or an insurance company as they wait for death. Unless they get sick or are very, very old that they can't do anything, I think people should be allowed to add value. It is healthy and biblical.

> A human runs out of time not potential, so they should be left to work until they die if they are able

The concept of stopping work at a certain age is foreign to God and it is contrary to Biblical teaching. A human runs out of time not potential, so they should be left to work until they die if they are able. Even if they live for a thousand years, a human being still has more potential left than what they have expressed.

Therefore, what do I mean when I say we have to aim for retirement if I am against the concept of retirement as we know it? You may be wondering by now why this chapter is called "Aim for Retirement", but I am seemingly going against what we know as "retirement"? No, I am not attacking retirement as it is shown in the Bible. I am attacking, if at all I am, the concept that we have come to call retirement.

The passages of scripture that we started this chapter with gives a clue as to what retirement is. Two things that are very important about retirement are:

First, retirement has nothing to do with stopping work. God does not expect anyone to stop adding value to society even in their old age. Adding value does not mean only doing work that requires hard labor.

It should be noted here, that the system of retirement we use was implemented during the industrial revolution. It was definitely required that someone should stop working at a certain age because of the type of work that was done. However, that has not been the original plan of God. No one should stop working.

Research shows that those who stop adding value to society, end up dead in a few years. A human being always wants to feel useful. That was how we were designed. To stop working is to operate outside our design.

Second, the scripture shows us that finishing what God was creating does not mean stopping to work. The Bible says, "He finished the work He was doing and what He was creating", not that He stopped work. Our failure to see what is going on in these two phrases is responsible for our misconception about retirement.

God was creating a system. He had a blue print of a system He was busy creating, although, what He was doing involved work. Work here is not the main thing. Creation of a system is the main thing.

When God was done with the creation of a system, the Bible says, He rested from what He was doing and what He was creating. Finishing creating something is very different from stopping to work.

In John 5:14-17 we clearly see that even on the same day that Genesis says God rested, Jesus shows us that God was still at work. What is the difference between the work in Genesis and the work in John? The work in Genesis was about creating a system to achieve something. While the work in John has to do with working in the system that was created. Every man and every woman should make it their aim to create a money system that they can use so that when they retire, they can continue to work.

Success Secrets from the Bible

I will use an example to illustrate what I am saying. A man works for 5 to 10 years creating a viable business that ends up running on its own without him. After a tough 10 years he creates a very successful business that gives him an income whether he works or not. At this time, we can call such a man someone who has retired.

Now, he doesn't have to stop working per say, he works not out of necessity but out of desire. He finished working, but he doesn't have to stop working in his system, just like God did. He created a world system, but He continues to work in it, although it is not every day that He has to take the sun up. He created a system to do that. There was a time there was no sun all together.

Another lady, who works as a manager at a law firm, decides to save up money over a period of 15 years. In these years she accumulates enough money that she invests into a real estate business. She buys herself five flats that pay her rental income of two times her current salary. Even if she may not quit her job at a law firm, this woman has retired because work to her is not out of necessity but out of desire. She created a money system that looks after her whether she works or not. So she doesn't have to stop working, but truth is she has retired.

> Retirement has nothing to do with accumulating millions of dollars in the bank. It means creating a system that gives you the income that you want to live the way you want without you having to work as a necessity.

Therefore, I advise you as a reader to consider aiming for retirement, not just for stopping working. I don't know which route you will take. But retirement simply means that you have created a working money system that brings you the income that you need to live the way you want to live without you having necessarily have to work. Retirement has nothing to do with accumulating millions of dollars in the bank. It means creating a system that gives you the income that you want to live the way you want without you having to work as a necessity.

Success Secrets from the Bible

I do subscribe to Robert Kiyosaki's definition of what an asset is. He says an asset is something that puts money in our pocket. Therefore, retirement is about creating, or acquiring an asset that gives us the amount of money we need to live the way we want to without you having to necessarily have to be involved in the acquiring of that money. The system we create, which Kiyosaki calls an asset is what produces that income.

If you say you need to live on $10,000 per month and you have an asset that gives you that, I call you retired. If you live on $20,000 but require work for that, and if your job is terminated that flow stops, I don't care how lavish your life looks like, the guy who has decided to retire on $10,000 is better off than you.

So, the ninth and last, success Secret from the Bible is "Aim for Retirement". Remember, retirement has nothing to do with stopping work. It has everything to do with creating a money system that works for us. We can then choose to work in it, do charity work, or travel the world. The choice is ours. But stopping to work to

Kenneth Mwale

wait for a cheque from government or an insurance company isn't God's idea of retirement.

## Other Books by Kenneth Mwale

Book a Keynote Speech

Organise a Workshop for your Church, Staff or Public one and ask Kenneth Mwale to come and facilitate

The Practical Truth Library

www.kennethmwale.com

kenmwale@gmail.com

+27 72 423 6990

www.ingramcontent.com/pod-product-compliance
Lightning Source LLC
Chambersburg PA
CBHW030714220526
45463CB00005B/2042